The Story of

Fossil Fuels

William B. Rice

Consultant

Catherine Hollinger, CID, CLIA
EPA WaterSense Partner
Environmental Consultant

Publishing Credits

Rachelle Cracchiolo, M.S.Ed., *Publisher*
Conni Medina, M.A.Ed., *Managing Editor*
Diana Kenney, M.A.Ed., NBCT, *Senior Editor*
Dona Herweck Rice, *Series Developer*
Robin Erickson, *Multimedia Designer*
Timothy Bradley, *Illustrator*

Image Credits: Cover, p.1 iStockC; p.19 Courtney
Patterson; p.14 dieKleinert / Alamy; p.15 Getty
Images/Cultura; pp.8, 9, 12, 14, 19, 20, 21, 22, 23,
25, 26, 32 iStock; p.28, 29 Janelle Bell-Martin; p.27
LOOK Die Bildagentur der Fotografen GmbH /
Alamy; p.12 M. I. Walker / Science Source; p.13
Mark A. Schneider / Science Source; pp.13, 31
Martin Shields / Science Source; p.11 Peter
Bowater / Alamy; p.13 Photo Researchers /
Science Source; p.7 Publiphoto / Science Source;
p.4 Walter Myers / Science Source; p.4 Wikimedia
Commons; all other images from Shutterstock.

Library of Congress Cataloging-in-Publication Data

Rice, William B. (William Benjamin), 1961- author.
  The story of fossil fuels / William B. Rice.
      pages cm
  Summary: "Everything needs energy to run. You get
energy from food. Cars also need energy. But cars don't
eat food--they use gasoline. Gasoline is made from fossil
fuels. Fossil fuels are used every day. Even roads for cars
are made from fossil fuels. Fossil fuels are a part of your
life more than you probably imagined."-- Provided by
publisher.
  Audience: Grades 4 to 6
  Includes index.
  ISBN 978-1-4807-4690-9 (pbk.)
1. Fossil fuels--Juvenile literature. 2. Natural resources--
Juvenile literature. I. Title.
  TP318.3.R52 2016
  333.8'2--dc23
                                    2014045213

Teacher Created Materials

5301 Oceanus Drive
Huntington Beach, CA 92649-1030
http://www.tcmpub.com

ISBN 978-1-4807-4690-9

Table of Contents

One Fine Day

Everywhere you look, the land is lush and green. Mosses and ferns bend and sway in the damp air. Giant insects buzz, and reptiles scratch as rain drips through the canopy of leaves overhead.

From a distance, a green winged creature darts closer. Its wings span a width of nearly a meter. It is the size of a modern seagull. It drifts through the trees. As it glides, it notices a giant cockroach on the rock below. The roach is unaware of a centipede crawling near— poisonous and two meters long. The winged insect flies past.

But the insect tires as it flies. It has lived long in this wild place, and now it looks for a place to rest. Its life is coming to an end. It is too tired to continue. Slowly it drifts to the ground below, the muddy bank of a flowing river.

The dragonfly-like creature of 350 million years ago is known as a *meganeura*.

There in the mud, the insect takes its last breath. The rain continues to fall and buries the insect's body deeper in the mud. Deeper, deeper it sinks. In time, its body **decomposes**. The roach and centipede do, too. Soon enough, the plants and trees die, and their rotting leaves and stems mix with the muddy goo.

Time passes. Days, months, and years go by. Decades and centuries begin to fly past. Then, millennia are gone. And finally millions of years.

The insect is not even a memory now. But its **remains** have combined with the remains of all the other creatures below Earth's surface. Heat and pressure have been constants. The mass has transformed over the hundreds of millions of years that have gone by. It has not only become solid rock but also a store of energy.

Until one fine day, a day just like today, a modern mining rig breaks through, and the solid store of energy sees the light of day....

Chickens or Eggs?

Certain animals needed the Carboniferous Era to evolve. During this time, eggs that could be laid safely on land developed—just like eggs from a chicken!

Carboniferous Era

The Carboniferous Era is part of the Paleozoic Era of geological time. It is known for the large underground layers of **coal** that were deposited then, from 359 to 299 million years ago. Below the surface of Earth, matter from millions of years ago transformed into today's fossil fuels.

The word *carboniferous* means "coal-bearing." The word contains two Latin words—*carbo*, meaning "coal," and *fero*, meaning "I bear" or "I carry."

What Are Fossil Fuels?

Fossil fuels are substances such as **petroleum**, coal, and **natural gas**. We use them every day. They are called *fossil fuels* because they are made from **organisms** that died and were buried under many layers of dirt and rock called **sediment**. They are fuels because they provide energy that powers most of our needs.

Petroleum is a fossil fuel that is made from very tiny organisms that lived in the oceans long ago. Coal is made from plants and animals that lived on land. Natural gas is made in both places, in oceans and on land. But all these fuels have one thing in common. The organisms that made them lived and died hundreds of millions of years ago.

Coal is a dark brown or black solid rock.

Natural gas is a clear gas that has no odor or taste.

Fossils

Fossils are the remains of prehistoric living things that have been preserved in rock or as a mold in rock.

The word *petroleum* comes from two Greek words. *Petro* is the word for "rock," and *oleum* is the word for "oil."

Petroleum varies in color from yellow to black.

All these fuels provide most of the energy demands for the world. Each is considered a **nonrenewable** resource. That means they are not easily renewed, or replenished. It will take many millions of years to renew them.

Not all petroleum is the same. Not all coal is the same. Not all natural gas is the same, either. Some are considered better than others. Some need more **refining**, or treatment. Some need less. And some have more energy per gallon than others.

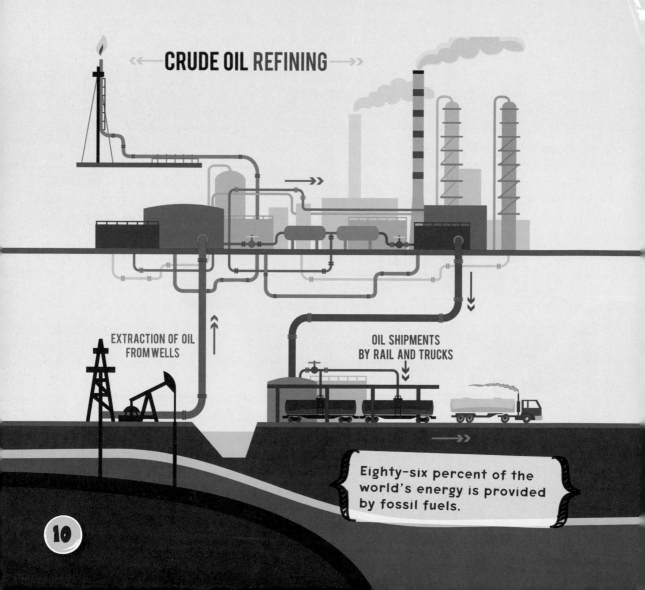

CRUDE OIL REFINING

EXTRACTION OF OIL FROM WELLS

OIL SHIPMENTS BY RAIL AND TRUCKS

Eighty-six percent of the world's energy is provided by fossil fuels.

oil refinery

Refining Oil

Another term often used for petroleum is *crude oil*. Crude oil usually refers to the substance that is pumped from the ground before it has been refined. *Crude* means "very simple and basic." The oil we see and use is much more complex than natural oil.

How Are Fossil Fuels Made?

Petroleum and natural gas are made from plants and animals that died hundreds of millions of years ago. Back then, very small plants and animals, much like the ones we know now, floated in the oceans. The plants are called *phytoplankton*. They were capable of photosynthesis just like other plants. The animals are called *zooplankton*. They ate other tiny animals. They also ate living and dead plants. Though tiny, there were billions of them in the oceans. Because they were living, their bodies held lots of sun energy. They also held energy from their food.

As they died, their bodies settled on the ocean bottoms. They piled up for millions of years. The piles got thicker over time. They got mixed and buried by sediments. The layers of sediments and dead things made pressure. They also made things very hot.

phytoplankton

Gasp!

Fossil fuels form during an anaerobic process. *Anaerobic* means there is no oxygen.

zooplankton

Types of Coal

There are three main kinds of coal.

Anthracite produces the most energy and burns the cleanest.

Bituminous coal has less energy and more pollutants when it burns.

Lignite has the least energy and the most pollutants.

Pressure and heat transformed the buried plants and animals. They were no longer solid but materials that could flow. In time, they became petroleum and natural gas. Movements in the earth pushed them closer to the surface.

Coal was made in a similar way but on land. Millions of years ago, there were swamps over large parts of Earth's surface. Lots of plants and animals lived there. As these organisms died, their bodies piled up on the ground. Years and years went by. More materials piled up thicker and thicker. Everything got buried deep underground. This created a hot, high-pressure environment. And that changed the materials into coal and natural gas.

Many years later, human beings came along. Humans learned how to get fossil fuels out of the ground. And they learned how to use the fuels for many different purposes.

Petroleum

How is petroleum formed? The process is simple.

First, plant and animal remains sink to the bottom of a body of water and are covered with mud.

High Risk, High Reward

People have been mining coal for thousands of years in much the same way they always have. It's dangerous work, but many people do it.

After years of pressure, the mud turns into layers of rock and the decaying plants and animals become liquid.

The liquid seeps up through porous rock. Porous rock has holes in it. When it finds a non-porous layer, it collects between the two to become oil and gas.

How Do We Use Fossil Fuels?

Since fossil fuels are made from plants and other once-living things, they can be burned. When we burn them, they give off heat that we can use. We can cook. We can power things. We can warm up.

Petroleum is used to make gasoline and diesel fuel. It is burned in the engines of cars, buses, trains, and airplanes. Burning the fuel gives vehicles power to move.

Petroleum is a very useful energy resource. It has a lot of concentrated energy. So, a little bit goes a long way. It is also easily **transported**. It can get from its source to places that need it without a lot of trouble. It is also easily used.

Coal is mainly burned at power plants to make electricity. The electricity is carried by power lines to businesses, factories, and houses. Long ago, people used coal to warm their homes. But that is not so much the case anymore.

In the United States alone, about 1,393 million liters (368 million gallons) of gasoline are used each day.

Running Low on Fuel

Fossil fuels are running out much faster than they can be made. Our current coal supply will only last about 1,500 years at the rate it's been used in the past. With only a 5 percent growth rate, it will last less than 100 years!

Big Coal in China

About 80 percent of China's electricity comes from coal. That is compared to only 30 percent of the world's electricity that comes from coal.

coal-fired power plant

Natural gas is burned at power plants to make electricity, too. The electricity is carried in the same way as it is in coal production. Natural gas is also used for cooking and heating. And it is used in many manufacturing processes. It is carried by pipelines to businesses, factories, and homes. In these places, it is burned. That is how we can use it for cooking and heating. It is also used to power cars and to make fertilizers for crops.

Plastic items are made from petroleum. These include car parts, toys, tools, TV sets, and cell phones. It even includes some clothing!

Without these fuels, we could not have the type of civilization we have. We could not live with the **industry** that we do. We certainly could not drive like we do. We could not even have the buildings, freeways, and roads that we have. And plane travel would be a thing of the past.

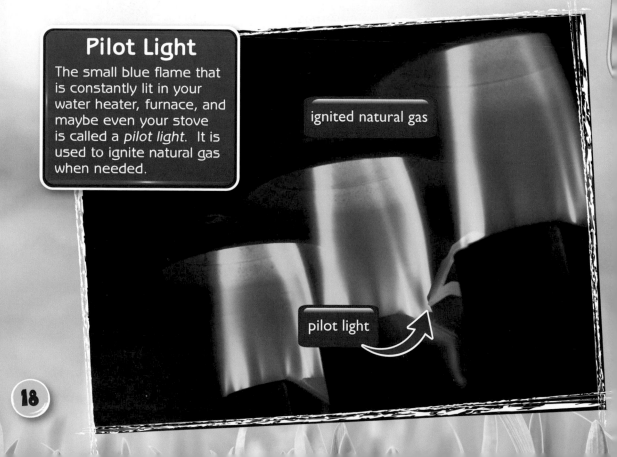

Pilot Light

The small blue flame that is constantly lit in your water heater, furnace, and maybe even your stove is called a *pilot light*. It is used to ignite natural gas when needed.

ignited natural gas

pilot light

Surprise!

Here are some of the more surprising products that use fossil fuels.

PETROLEUM
- crayons
- pillows
- aspirin
- CDs

NATURAL GAS
- plastic
- ammonia
- paint
- trash bags

COAL
- soap
- plastic
- tennis rackets
- mountain bikes

The Smell of Safety

Mercaptan is added to natural gas for our safety. It gives gas a smell that warns us when gas might be leaking.

The energy we get from fossil fuels actually comes from the sun. The plants that make up fossil fuels stored the sun's energy while they were living.

Where Do We Find Fossil Fuels Today?

Petroleum and natural gas are found below the ground in many parts of the world. But they are found in plenty in just a few places. These places are oil fields and natural gas fields. The largest fields are in the Middle East. There are also large fields in India, Brazil, and Mexico. Venezuela, Kazakhstan, and Russia also have large fields. The United States does, too.

Natural gas is also found where we find coal. Coal is mined in many parts of the world. Countries that have mined a lot of coal include the United Kingdom and Germany. France and Belgium have, too. Today, China and the United States are big producers of coal. India, Australia, and Russia also produce a lot. China produces more coal than any other country in the world. The United States is second when it comes to coal production.

The world's largest consumers of fossil fuels, such as the United States and China, are often the world's biggest polluters.

Mining for Chocolate

Try this experiment at home to see how the mining of fossil fuels affects the land.

1. Get a chocolate chip cookie and a toothpick.

2. Use the toothpick to carefully mine, or remove, the chocolate chips from the cookie.

3. How many chocolate chips were you able to extract? What happened to the rest of the cookie? Can you make any connections to mining and the land?

Fossil Fuel States

In the United States, big producers of natural gas include Alaska, California, Pennsylvania, and Texas. Big producers of coal include Pennsylvania, West Virginia, Wyoming, Kentucky, and Illinois.

natural oil well

Extraction and Refining

Oil is a liquid and natural gas is a gas. They are able to flow, so they are pumped out of the ground using oil and gas wells. The oil or gas is extracted, or pulled, from Earth. To make the wells, holes are drilled deep into the ground. Then, pipes that are like big, long straws are placed in the holes.

Petroleum is made of hundreds of chemicals. To make it usable, it is processed and cleaned at a **refinery**. The chemicals are separated from each other. Then, they are transported for use or more processing.

Natural gas is treated at a processing plant. The gas is cleaned and processed to separate out chemicals. Then, the gas is transported for use.

Coal is a solid. It is removed from underground by mining. To mine the coal, large pits or tunnels are dug underground. To make it usable, coal is processed at a preparation plant. It is cleaned and crushed. The pieces are sorted by size and loaded for transport.

In Others Words, Fracking

Certain rocks make it difficult to get petroleum and natural gas out of the ground. In that case, a complex and costly process called *hydraulic fracturing* is used. It is commonly known as **fracking**. In this process, fluids are pumped into the ground under very high pressure. This fractures the rocks and releases the petroleum and natural gas. They are then pumped out as usual.

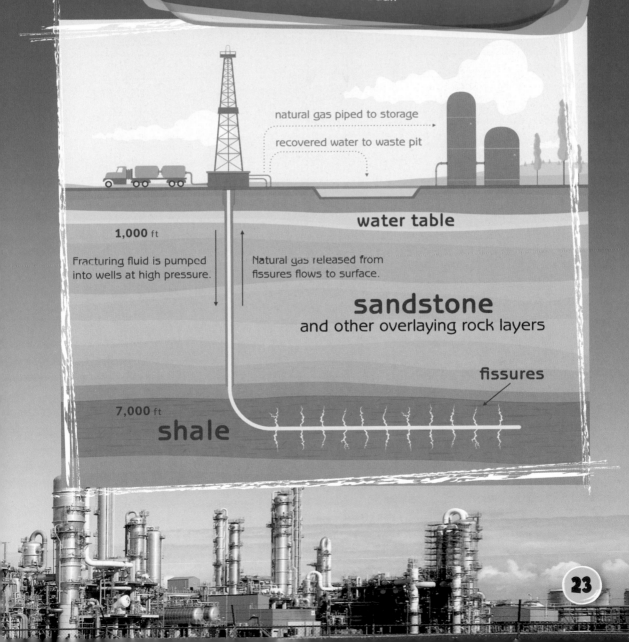

natural gas piped to storage

recovered water to waste pit

water table

1,000 ft

Fracturing fluid is pumped into wells at high pressure.

Natural gas released from fissures flows to surface.

sandstone
and other overlaying rock layers

fissures

7,000 ft

shale

How Much More?

Fossil fuels are nonrenewable resources. That means the supply has a limit. Once the fuels are used, there are no more.

M. King Hubbert was an earth scientist who worked in the oil industry. He studied oil fields, gas fields, and more. Based on his studies, he found that all oil wells have a regular life span. They start off pumping small amounts at first. Then, they work up to pumping their maximum for a while. Gradually they taper off to small amounts again. Then, they go dry. Hubbert plotted this span on a graph. It became well known as *Hubbert's Curve*.

Upon further study, Hubbert found that this curve could be applied to whole fields, whole countries, and even the world. He predicted that worldwide oil production would reach a peak around the year 2000. Many people doubted his ideas. But all oil wells and fields have followed the pattern he found.

Gasohol

Scientists have long been developing alternative energy for fossil fuels. Gasohol is made from gasoline combined with ethyl alcohol. Ethyl alcohol leaves much less contamination than gasoline does, and it is renewable.

Coming Up

Current predictions say that Hubbert's Curve was a little off. Experts predict that oil production will peak between 2010 and 2020. They say that it could peak as late as 2030, but any later is not likely.

Production

build-up phase

maximum peak

accelerated decline

steady decline

slow decline

tail

Time

The supply of fossil fuels on planet Earth is limited. Someday, it will be too difficult, too expensive, or not worth the effort to extract more fossil fuels.

It is important for us all to make wise choices and use our resources carefully. We can think of fossil fuels like a big lottery payoff. The amount won is huge and can last a long time. But if we actually spend it, it cannot last forever. Knowing that, how can we make better use of our resources today? How can we plan the best for the future? Will future generations have what we have and be able to do what we do? How will they fuel their world?

Thinking Differently

Imagine that a mall only filled its vending machines once a year. Everyone would need to work together to share the snacks and make them last throughout the year. That's how nonrenewable resources work.

Re-creating the Sun

Our energy comes from the sun. People have tried for many years to mimic the sun's output to create new energy sources. We are trying to balance the cost with the energy produced.

solar power plant

Think Like a Scientist

How are fossils created? Experiment and find out!

What to Get

- 3 slices of bread (one white, one wheat, one rye)
- clear drinking straw
- gummy candy
- heavy books
- knife
- paper towels

What to Do

1 Pull the crust off all three slices of bread.

2 Place the slice of white bread on top of a paper towel. Put three gummy candies on top of the white bread.

3 Repeat Step 2 with the rye and wheat bread. Stack the slices of bread and layer them together. Observe the gummy candies. Record your observations on a chart like this one.

Step	Observation	Drawing

4 Put a paper towel over the stack of bread. Place two heavy books on top. Leave the stack for three days.

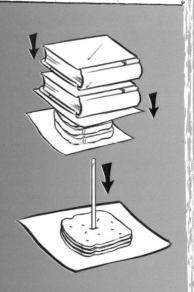

5 On the third day, remove the books and paper towel. Push a drinking straw through the layers to take a sample of the core. Record your observations.

6 Have an adult help you cut your rock layers in half. Record your observations.

7 Peel the bread apart. What do you notice about the gummies? Record your observations.

Glossary

coal—a nonrenewable fossil fuel made from peat

decomposes—slowly breaks down

fracking—properly called hydraulic fracturing, a complex process in which liquids are injected at high pressures underground to crack rocks and release crude oil and natural gas

industry—business

mercaptan—a chemical added to natural gas to give it odor for safety

natural gas—gas that is taken from underground and is used as fuel

nonrenewable—cannot be replaced

organisms—living things

petroleum—an oily, flammable liquid created in the earth from decaying organisms; used as a source of fuel

refinery—a place where crude oil is processed to make petroleum products such as gasoline, diesel fuel, and jet fuel

refining—the processing of crude oil to make products

remains—the leftover material after something has died

sediment—small pieces of rock, such as sand, gravel, and dust

transported—carried from one place to another

Index

Your Turn!

Using Fossil Fuels

How do you use fossil fuels each day? It's good to be aware of the energy you use, especially energy that is nonrenewable. Make a list of everything you do or use in a day that uses fossil fuels or was made with fossil fuels. How big is your list? Now, imagine what life would be like without gasoline, natural gas, or electricity. Are there any ways you can use less energy?